PIERCE ARROW FIRE APPARATUS

1979 THROUGH 1998 PHOTO ARCHIVE

Steven Hagy

Iconografix
Photo Archive Series

Iconografix
PO Box 446
Hudson, Wisconsin 54016 USA

Iconografix books are offered at a discount when sold in quantity for promotional use. Businesses or organizations seeking details should write to the Marketing Department, Iconografix, at the above address.

Library of Congress Card Number: 99-76051

ISBN 1-58388-023-2

00 01 02 03 04 05 06 5 4 3 2 1

Printed in the United States of America

Cover and book design by Shawn Glidden

Copy editing by Dylan Frautschi

On the cover: Lexington, Kentucky has this 1987 Pierce Arrow 105-foot aerial with Pierce serial #E 3517. The "Spirit of the Bluegrass" is in service as Aerial 1. *Steve Hagy.*

Iconografix Inc. exists to preserve history through the publication of notable photographic archives and the list of titles under the Iconografix imprint is constantly growing. Transportation enthusiasts should be on the Iconografix mailing list and are invited to write and ask for a catalog, free of charge.

Authors and editors in the field of transportation history are invited to contact the Editorial Department at Iconografix, Inc., PO Box 446, Hudson, WI 54016. We require a minimum of 120 photographs per subject. We prefer subjects narrow in focus, e.g., a specific model, railroad, or racing venue. Photographs must be of high quality, suited to large format reproduction.

PREFACE

The histories of machines and mechanical gadgets are contained in the books, journals, correspondence, and personal papers stored in libraries and archives throughout the world. Written in tens of languages, covering thousands of subjects, the stories are recorded in millions of words.

Words are powerful. Yet, the impact of a single image, a photograph or an illustration, often relates more than dozens of pages of text. Fortunately, many of the libraries and archives that house the words also preserve the images.

In the *Photo Archive Series,* Iconografix reproduces photographs and illustrations selected from public and private collections. The images are chosen to tell a story—to capture the character of their subject. Reproduced as found, they are accompanied by the captions made available by the archive.

The Iconografix *Photo Archive Series* is dedicated to young and old alike, the enthusiast, the collector and anyone who, like us, is fascinated by "things" mechanical.

ACKNOWLEDGMENTS

It would have been impossible to produce this book without the assistance of my friends. Their names are shown after each caption. I thank you all. Also, I thank my wife Melody for her support and patience while I completed this book.

This 1979 delivery to Kansas City, Kansas is believed to be the first Pierce Arrow built. Pumper 5 has a 1500-gpm (gallons per minute) Waterous pump and a 500-gallon booster tank. Carrying Pierce serial #E 0130, this rig was the beginning of hundreds of rigs to be built with the Pierce Arrow name over a period of more than 20 years. *Steve Loftin.*

INTRODUCTION

Pierce Arrow. In the 1920s if you had mentioned this name you would have been discussing a manufacturer of high quality automobiles and trucks. Mention this name today, and firefighters everywhere will know that you are speaking of the high quality fire apparatus built by Pierce Manufacturing.

This volume chronicles a small portion of the apparatus constructed by Pierce Manufacturing of Appleton, Wisconsin. Founded in 1913, the shop originally opened and began business by converting automobiles into utility-type vehicles. Soon, truck bodies were added to the product line. During the 1930s the first fire apparatus bodies were constructed. For over 20 years production of fire apparatus grew and became an increasingly larger portion of the output. Pierce found a niche in the market during the 1960s when they began producing bodies for the newly conceived snorkel, which was much in favor with departments across the country.

Custom pumpers were added to the line up in the early 1970s with the introduction of the Fire Marshall series. Based on GMC and Oshkosh chassis, these rigs were equipped with Truck Cab Manufacturers' (Cincinnati) cabs. In 1979 Pierce introduced the Arrow. Like the earlier Fire Marshall series, the Arrow was constructed on chassis assembled by other manufacturers. Oshkosh and Duplex chassis were available for the Arrow.

An all-aluminum cab that had 88 inches of interior width was a standard feature on the Arrow. The rig was constructed with a 178-inch wheelbase utilizing a Detroit Diesel 6V-92TA, 335 HP engine, an Allison HT-740 4-speed automatic transmission, and Ross power steering.

The body was made using galvanneal steel with solid, double panel doors and full, rear-wheel innerliners. Waterous pumps were used with capacities available from 1000 to 2000 gpm. Booster tanks were available in standard sizes of 500, 750, and 1000 gallons. This made the Arrow a first class rig with features and construction that rivaled any manufacturer in the industry.

The Arrow proved to be a well-liked model among departments all across the United States and in some foreign countries too. Since most fire apparatus is built to different specifications, additional options were offered as the demand for Pierce Arrow apparatus increased. Four-door crew cabs became available in the early 1980s. Hydraulic ladder racks, top-mounted pump panels, and foam systems are among many preferred features.

In 1983 production of the Arrow began by using chassis constructed by Pierce. They were now delivering a true custom, single source fire engine. The popularity of the Arrow continued to increase and with the demand for custom chassis apparatus, Pierce began adding new chassis types for their firefighting customers from the mid-1980s through the 1990s. The Dash, Lance, Javelin, Saber, and Quantum would eventually be added to the product line offered by Pierce Manufacturing.

Inside of this volume you will find a representation of the full range of apparatus crafted and delivered by Pierce as the Arrow. Most of the deliveries are of ground-up, factory-built Arrows. A few are of rehabbed rigs that have been rebuilt using the Arrow cab. The rigs shown run the gamut of types of fire equipment in service today. Pumpers, tankers, acrials, snorkels, and heavy rescue rigs have been built on the Arrow chassis.

Towns both large and small have purchased Pierce Arrows to protect their citizens. I have strived to include a cross section of apparatus in states from the Atlantic to the Pacific, as Pierce delivers apparatus in every state of the Union.

For those of you that are interested in fire engine history, I must make note of SPAAMFAA. The Society for the Preservation and Appreciation of Antique Motor Fire Apparatus in America was founded in 1958. Thousands of members make up more than 50 local chapters of the Society. Among the benefits of joining is the receipt of two excellent quarterly publications. *Enjine! Enjine!* magazine traces fire engine history and restoration through interesting articles about antique and vintage apparatus. *The Silver Trumpet* is a newsletter that provides restoration tips and tidbits, and lists fire engine musters, flea markets, and other events of interest in North America. Membership information is available from SPAAMFAA at: P.O. Box 2005, Syracuse, New York 13220-2005.

You can also learn more about SPAAMFAA on the Internet by viewing their web site at www.spaamfaa.org.

This demonstrator was shown all over the U.S. For many people, this was their first look at the new Pierce Arrow. Although rather Spartan in appearance by current standards, this rig was as good as it gets in 1980. The wide, aluminum cab and galvanneal body were standard features on the Arrow. Serial #E 0134 has a 1250-gpm pump and a 500-gallon tank. Where this piece was eventually delivered is unknown. *Steve Hagy.*

Woodward Township at Linden, Pennsylvania has this 1980 Arrow in service as Engine 2. A 1500-gpm pump is operated from a top-mounted panel, and 1,000 gallons of water are carried on this rig. *Rick Rudisill.*

Ladder 5 in Des Moines, Iowa has this 1980 delivery. Equipped with a 100-foot aerial built by LTI (Ladder Towers Inc.) of Ephrata, Pennsylvania, this big rig also has a 1500-gpm pump. LTI supplied aerial devices used on Pierce apparatus for many years. *Paul Barrett.*

Although four-door enclosed cab apparatus is taken for granted today, when this pumper was shipped to Anoka, Minnesota in 1980, it was the exception to the rule. This is one of the earliest, if not the first, deliveries of a Pierce Arrow with a four-door cab. This rig has a 1250-gpm pump and carries 500 gallons of water. *Paul Barrett.*

An Oshkosh chassis was used for this 1981 delivery to Dalton, Illinois. Truck 1442 has a 75-foot Tele-Squrt, 1250-gpm pump, and 200-gallon tank mounted on a tandem rear axle chassis. Serial #E 0911. *Jack Connors.*

This rig is ready for a fire! Many volunteer fire companies carry gear for members on board the rig. Fair Haven, New Jersey is a fine example of this. Coats and helmets are stored above the compartments of the pumper. This 1981 delivery has a 1250-gpm pump and 500-gallon tank. The crisp white paint on this rig makes it shine. *Scott Mattson.*

The Pearl River Hook & Ladder Company of Pearl River, New York operated this 1981 Arrow. This rig has a 100-foot LTI rear-mount aerial and is also equipped with a 250-gpm booster pump and a 375-gallon tank. After faithfully serving in Pearl River, this rig was sold to the Consolidated Fire Protection District that protects the towns of North Auburn, Lone Star, and Ophir, California. *Neal Van Deusen.*

Millard, Nebraska placed this rig in service during 1981. Constructed on an Oshkosh chassis, this piece has a 50-foot Tele-Squrt aerial device, a 1500-gpm pump, and a 500-gallon booster tank. Serial #E 1140. *Chuck Madderom.*

A 100-foot aerial tower is in service with Truck 20 in Dallas, Texas. LTI built the tower for this 1981 Arrow, which is serial #E 0885. *Eric Hansen.*

When you don't have a hydrant, you have to bring the water with you! The Troy Fire Protection District of Shorewood, Illinois operates this pumper-tanker. 2,500 gallons of water are on board, along with a 1250-gpm pump. Although most early Pierce Arrow deliveries were on Oshkosh chassis, Duplex chassis were also available. Delivered in 1982 and carrying serial #E 1642, this lime green monster was built on a Duplex. *Jack Connors.*

Canton, Mississippi Fire Department operates this 1982 Arrow as Engine 81. Constructed on an Oshkosh chassis, this rig is equipped with a 1750-gpm Waterous pump and a 500-gallon booster tank. Serial #E 1600. *Steve Hagy.*

Snorkels were also constructed using Pierce Arrow chassis. Oshtemo Township, Michigan placed this Oshkosh-Pierce in service during 1982. Equipped with a 1500-gpm pump, 200-gallon tank, and an 85-foot snorkel, this rig can easily reach up and over the roof of a building. Serial #E 1563. *Garry Kadzielawski.*

Blauvelt, New York is the proud owner of this 1983 Pierce Arrow. Serial #E 1997 has a 2000-gpm pump and a 500-gallon tank. *Neal Van Deusen.*

Many fire departments name their apparatus in honor of former members or prominent citizens of their communities. This 1983 Arrow in Evansville, Indiana is named for Walter J. Hess. Engine 4 is a 1250-gpm pumper with a 500-gallon tank and serial #E 1875. *Greg Stapleton.*

This interesting looking rig is in service at Marcellus, New York. Built in 1983, it has a 1500-gpm pump, a 1000-gallon tank, and a 55-foot Fire Stix aerial device. Serial #E 1961. *Mark Redman.*

The Great Barrington Fire Department of Housatonic, Massachusetts operates this 1983 Arrow as Engine 6. The rig is equipped with a 1000-gpm pump and is serial #E 2123. Note that the body is higher than normal to accommodate the 1000-gallon booster tank on the rig. *Neal Van Deusen.*

Although a fixture in many departments years ago, quads are rarely used in the fire service today. Kenmore, New York has this 1983 Arrow quad. A quad is a piece of apparatus that has the equipment needed to perform four primary firefighting functions. This rig has a pump, hose, a complete set of ground ladders, and carries water. Although most pumpers carry these items, they do not carry the full set of ground ladders that are on this rig. Note the extension ladder on the side of the rig. The body of the rig is also built up to accommodate the additional ground ladders that are accessible from the rear. This piece has a 1250-gpm pump and 500-gallon tank. Serial #E 1941. *Dan Martin.*

Many departments extend the service life of their apparatus by having them rebuilt. Huber Heights, Ohio purchased this 1952 American LaFrance 100-foot aerial from Ardmore, Pennsylvania. In 1984 the rig was sent to Pierce where it was completely refurbished. Bearing serial #F 1271, this apparatus has the appearance of a new rig. *John Denney.*

Truck 1 in Kansas City, Kansas has this midship-mount aerial. The aerial is a 100-foot LTI and was one of a pair of these rigs delivered during 1984. Serial #E 2233-01. *Steve Loftin*.

Delivered in 1984 for the Palos Heights Fire Protection District, Illinois, this rig is equipped with a 1250-gpm pump, 300-gallon tank, and a 75-foot Tele-Squrt. Most 75-foot Tele-Squrts are delivered on chassis with tandem rear axles. The large front overhang on this piece is due to the use of a single rear axle. Serial #E 2148. *Jack Connors.*

Randolph Township Fire Department near Union, Ohio had this 1984 Arrow pumper-tanker in service. A 2500-gallon tank and 1750-gpm pump are on Engine 42. Serial #E 2404. *John Denney.*

Moorhead, Minnesota operates this 1985 delivery as engine 901, with a 1250-gpm pump and 750-gallon booster tank. The enclosed pump panel gives this rig the look of a rescue truck. *Paul Barrett.*

Occasionally other manufacturers of fire apparatus use Pierce Arrow chassis for their rigs. Such is the case with this heavy rescue for Seaford, Delaware. The body on this rig was constructed by Saulsbury of Tully, New York and the chassis is Pierce serial #E 2687. *Rick Rudisill.*

Many fire departments prefer to use top-mount pump control panels. Hardeeville, South Carolina operates this 1985 Pierce Arrow with a 1500-gpm pump and a 750-gallon tank. *Rick Rudisill.*

Industrial fire departments also use Pierce Arrow apparatus. Lockheed Aircraft of Burbank, California has this 1985 model in service. Engine 2 is equipped with a 1500-gpm pump, 500-gallon tank, and a 35-gallon foam tank. Serial #E 3097. *Chuck Madderom.*

Snorkel 1 in Saddle Brook, New Jersey is a 1985 Arrow with a 75-foot snorkel. This rig also has a 1000-gpm pump and 250-gallon booster tank. Serial #E 2520. *Neal Van Duesen.*

This 1500-gpm pumper at Elsmere, Delaware is equipped with a 54-foot Squrt. This versatile heavy stream appliance allows water to be directed over and into a burning building. A 500-gallon booster tank is also on this rig that was delivered in 1985. *Scott Mattson*.

Red fire apparatus with a white cab roof is very popular. Billings, Montana operates this 1985 Arrow quint with a 1500-gpm pump, 500-gallon tank, and a 55-foot aerial. Like many fire departments, Billings uses their apparatus for emergency medical service, rescue response to automobile accidents, and a wide range of other emergencies. *Leo Duliba.*

Ely, Nevada is home to this rig. Engine 7 has a 1500-gpm pump and a 2000-gallon tank. This all-white, 1985 addition to the E.F.D. is serial #E 2773. *Garry Kadzielawski.*

This rig is a bit unusual. Denham Springs, Louisiana operates this 1985 Pierce Arrow as Engine 3. In 1993 the body was replaced by Ferrara Fire Apparatus, which is located just a few miles from this town. It is equipped with a 1500-gpm pump and a 1000-gallon tank. Serial #E 2878. *Steve Hagy.*

Engine Company 11 in Charleston, South Carolina is seen here with their lime green Pierce Arrow. This 1986 delivery has a 1250-gpm pump and a 500-gallon tank. *Byron Brown.*

A 75-foot aerial is mounted on this 1986 Arrow for Council Bluffs, Iowa. 300 gallons of water are on board, along with a 1500-gpm pump. *Paul Barrett.*

With the use of large diameter hose, departments increasingly order rigs with greater pumping capacity. South Media, Pennsylvania has this 1986 Arrow in service with a 1750-gpm pump and a 500-gallon tank. Serial #E 2743. *Rick Rudisill.*

Sometimes components from an older rig are used in the construction of a new one. South Haven, Michigan had their rig delivered in 1986 with a 1500-gpm pump and a 1000-gallon tank. The 50-foot Tele-Squrt was remounted from another piece to this one. Serial #F 1721. *Jack Connors.*

Truck 255 at the Washington County Fire District #1 near Portland, Oregon is assigned this 1986 Pierce Arrow. Equipped with a 75-foot rear-mount aerial, the rig is serial #E 3111. *Bill Hattersley.*

Many large cities operate Pierce Arrow apparatus in their fleets. The Indianapolis, Indiana Fire Department uses this 1986 model as Engine 27, with a 1500-gpm pump and top-mount controls. It also carries 500 gallons of water. *Steve Hagy.*

This heavy rescue is in service at Ponderosa, Texas. Rescue 61 carries gear to handle virtually any type of entrapment or extrication situation. This 1986 delivery is serial #E 3143. *Eric Hansen.*

This 1987 Arrow pumper was operated by the Withamsville, Ohio Fire Department. Equipped with a 1500-gpm pump and a 750-gallon tank, it is serial #E 3014. This rig is now painted white and is in service with the Union Township Fire Department that is a consolidation of the North Union and Withamsville departments in Clermont County, Ohio. *Steve Hagy.*

Maui County, Hawaii operates this quint as Ladder 3 at Ho'olako. This 1987 delivery to paradise has a 1250-gpm pump and a 75-foot aerial on a tandem rear axle Arrow chassis. *Dennis Maag.*

Prince George County, Virginia has this 1987 Arrow as Engine 710. A 1250-gpm pump and a 750-gallon booster tank are used on serial #E 3489. The pictures in this book would not have been possible without the cooperation of firefighters across the country. My thanks to everyone who took the time to position a rig for a visiting photographer. *George Reichhardt.*

Chesterfield, Missouri provides protection to a small airport with this big rig. This 1987 purchase has a 1500-gpm pump, 1500-gallon tank, and a 200-gallon foam tank. Note the roof-mounted foam discharge nozzle. Serial #E 3328. *Dennis Maag.*

The Cornhusker State is the home to this 1987 Pierce Arrow. Engine 32 has a 1500-gpm pump and a 750-gallon booster tank and protects the town of Bellevue, Nebraska. *Paul Barrett.*

The Chemical Fire Co. No. 1 of Hummelstown, Pennsylvania operates this quint. A 75-foot aerial, 1250-gpm pump, and 300-gallon tank are on board serial #E 3382, which was received in 1987. *Rick Rudisill.*

Midship-mounted aerials provide a shorter overall height that makes them easier to fit in older stations with lower doors and ceilings. This style of apparatus is seldom seen on the Pierce Arrow chassis. East Wallingford, Connecticut operates this 1987 model as Ladder 8, which utilizes a 1975 American LaFrance 100-foot aerial. Serial #F 1924. *Mark Redman.*

Meridian, Mississippi has this 1987 delivery in service as Engine 7. Equipped with a 1000-gpm pump and a 750-gallon tank, it carries serial #E 3889. Like many towns, Meridian is a repeat customer that has purchased several Pierce pumpers. *Steve Hagy.*

A unique rig is this 1987 Arrow with a 55-foot snorkel. Squad 2 of the Memphis, Tennessee Fire Department operates this unit. Memphis has a long-standing tradition of naming their apparatus. This piece is named the "Frank B. Gianotti Jr.," and is marked with serial #E 3821. *George Reichhardt.*

In 1987 the St. Louis, Missouri Fire Department replaced all of their engine companies with quint-type apparatus. Among the rigs purchased to accomplish this were 15 Pierce Arrow's with 50-foot Tele-Squrts. These units were also equipped with 1500-gpm pumps, 500-gallon tanks, and 15-gallon foam tanks. Engine 11 is seen here with their rig, serial #E 3749-01. *Steve Hagy.*

Skokie, Illinois operates this 105-foot rear-mount aerial as Truck 18. Like many fire engines today, this 1988 model was sent back to the factory for rehab work after being in service for many years. Skokie firefighter Garry Kadzielawski photographed his department's rig. Serial #E 3880.

This is another rig where appearances can be deceiving. This piece was built in 1973 by Pierce on a Hendrickson model FTCO-2070 chassis. In 1988 the rig was completely rebuilt as an Arrow. Elgin, Alabama currently operates this unit as Engine 1. The rig is equipped with a 1250-gpm Waterous pump and a 750-gallon booster tank. Serial #F 1828 was originally in service at Hinsdale, Illinois. *Steve Hagy.*

This impressive looking machine is located in Ft. Loramie, Ohio. Carrying 2,500 gallons of water and a 1250-gpm pump, this rig is proudly posed in front of the local high school soon after acceptance in 1988. Serial #E 3986. *Steve Hagy.*

Top-mount control panels are a popular option for Pierce Arrow apparatus. Engine 4 in Kingman, Arizona is in service with a 1988 delivery. Serial #E 4304 is equipped with a 1500-gpm pump and a 750-gallon tank. *Chuck Madderom.*

Bowling Green, Kentucky has several pieces of Pierce apparatus on the roster, including this 1988 model. This 1250-gpm pumper with 500-gallon tank carries serial #E 4319 and was operating as Engine 4 when photographed. *Jerry Sudduth.*

The late Byron Brown photographed this 1988 Arrow with 85-foot snorkel while traveling through Raleigh, North Carolina. Notice the intricate RFD in gold leaf on the door. Paint schemes and lettering can really create a very striking appearance for a fire engine.

This rig is painted lime green with a white cab roof, and has blue reflective striping. East Longmeadow, Massachusetts operates this 1988 purchase as Ladder 1. It carries Pierce serial #E 4070 and is equipped with a 1250-gpm pump, 300-gallon tank, and 105-foot aerial. *Mark Redman.*

Tandem rear axles support the weight of the 105-foot aerial on this job for the Menlo Park Fire District of California. Truck 1's apparatus is serial #E 4328 and was delivered late in 1988. *Chuck Madderom.*

On the other end of the scale from the Menlo Park rig is this 75-foot rear-mount aerial. Operated by Irving, Texas as Truck 2, this 1989 model was constructed on a standard pumper chassis. The shorter wheelbase should make for a highly maneuverable rig. *Eric Hansen.*

East Point, Georgia runs with this 1989 Arrow at their headquarters station. It has a 1250-gpm pump with top-mount controls and a 750-gpm booster tank. Air-conditioning was beginning to become a feature on much apparatus purchased, and this rig is so equipped. Serial #E 4767. *Steve Hagy.*

Buffalo, New York has used several Pierce rigs over the years. Delivered in 1989, this heavy rescue with a walk-in rear body style is operated as Rescue 1. Serial #E 5176. *Dan Martin.*

Nashua, New Hampshire operates this 1500-gpm pumper as Engine 4. This 1989 delivery has a 750-gallon booster tank, 60-gallon foam tank, and a Mars siren mounted prominently on the front bumper. Serial #E 4854. *Jack Connors*.

Take a look at the cab on this rig and you know immediately that there is something different here. The Red, White, & Blue Volunteer Fire Rescue of Breckenridge, Colorado operates a pair of these pumpers that were built on four-wheel drive Arrow chassis. Another unusual feature of these 1989 rigs is a 1250-gallon booster tank to go with the 1500-gpm pump. Engine 616 is serial #E 4571-01. *Dennis Maag.*

The city of Jackson in eastern Kentucky has this 1989 model quint on the roster. The "Pride of the Mountains" has a 1500-gpm pump, 200-gallon tank, and 105-foot aerial. Serial #E 4555. *Steve Hagy.*

The 1500-gallon tank on this rig is rather apparent. Pleasant Prairie, Wisconsin operates this 1990 arrival that is also equipped with a 1500-gpm pump. Serial #E 5549. *George Reichhardt.*

Many towns operate Tele-Squrts as ladder apparatus. Hualapai Valley, Arizona uses this 1990 Pierce with a 50-foot Tele-Squrt, 1250-gpm pump, and 500-gallon tank. Serial #E 5366. *Chuck Madderom.*

By 1990, high side-compartments were a feature found on most pumpers delivered. Engine 1 in Wilmington, Delaware uses this 1500-gpm rig with a 500-gallon tank and 54-foot Squrt. The lack of the compartments gives this engine a low, lean look that is quite attractive. *Rick Rudisill.*

The Old Bridge V.F.D. of East Brunswick, New Jersey operates this 110-foot aerial tower that went to service in 1990. *Scott Mattson.*

Midship-mount aerial trucks haven't disappeared completely from the fire service. Danbury, Connecticut uses this 1990 Arrow with a 105-foot aerial as Truck 2. Serial #E 5742. *Neal Van Deusen.*

This quint for Pocatello, Idaho Engine 2 left the factory painted all white. After delivery, the rig was painted in a color scheme to match Idaho's license plates that were issued for that states centennial in 1990. Serial #E 5535 has a 1500-gpm pump, 500-gallon tank, and 55-foot aerial. *Bill Hattersley.*

The North Lake Tahoe Fire District, Nevada sees plenty of snow in their response area. This 1990 Arrow 4 x 4 has a 1500-gpm pump, 750-gallon tank, and serial #E 5759. *Garry Kadzielawski.*

Warr Acres, Oklahoma has this 1500-gpm pumper in service. The rig is equipped with a 750-gallon tank and top-mount pump controls. Engine 23 was built in 1990. Serial #E 5781. *Steve Loftin*.

Pierce apparatus is also delivered outside of the United States. Many Canadian deliveries had the apparatus body constructed by Superior Fire Apparatus of Red Deer, Alberta as is on this rig. Engine 2 in Richmond, British Columbia has this 1990 delivery with a 1750-gpm pump and 400-gallon tank. Serial #E 5773-01. *Bill Hattersley.*

Most paint jobs with a different color cab roof have the color change occur a couple of inches below the window. Lower Allen Township, Pennsylvania had the white paint on this rig brought down to the trim strip at mid-door. It gives the rig a very distinctive appearance. This 1990 model has a 1750-gpm pump and a 500-gallon tank. Serial #E 5509. *Rick Rudisill.*

Another very noticeable change in paint is the use of more non-traditional colors. This 1990 Arrow at Liberty, Kentucky is painted white-over-blue with a white reflective stripe. A 1500-gpm pump and 750-gallon tank round out the package on serial #E 5837. *Jerry Sudduth.*

Gary, Indiana purchased several Arrow pumpers in 1990. Engine 12 is seen in front of quarters with their 1500-gpm job. A 500-gallon booster tank is on this rig with serial #E 5830-01. Gary apparatus features a blue cab roof over a red body. *Jack Connors*.

Home sweet home! Pierce Manufacturing constructed this rig for Appleton, Wisconsin. The A.F.D. operates a pair of these 105-foot rear-mount aerials that were purchased in 1991. This is the rig assigned to Truck 341. Serial #E 6474-01. *Greg Stapleton.*

The West Valley Fire Department has this 1500-gpm quint in service. Truck 72 has 300 gallons of water and a 75-foot aerial. Serial #E 6095 is on this 1991 delivery to Utah. *Bill Hattersley.*

A 1991 model, this Arrow rolls with the Mauricetown Fire Company of Commercial Township, New Jersey. Tanker 12-02 has a 1250-gpm pump and a 2500-gallon tank. *Scott Mattson.*

Los Angeles County, California added 16 Arrow pumpers to the roster in 1991. Engine 106 has a 1000-gpm pump and a 500-gallon tank. These rigs were among the first delivered with grilles to allow for better air circulation to the engine. Serial #E 6327-04. *Chuck Madderom.*

This 1991 delivery is in service at Nichols Hills, Oklahoma. A 1250-gpm pump and a 750-gallon tank were specified for this rig. Serial #E 6335. *Steve Loftin.*

The United States Naval Academy at Annapolis, Maryland is protected by this 1991 addition. Serial #E 5917-02 is one of eleven similar rigs purchased by the Navy that year. This rig is equipped with a 1000-gpm pump, 500-gallon tank, and a 65-foot Tele-Squrt. *Jack Connors.*

Engine Co. 9 in Lafayette, Louisiana has this air-conditioned 1991 Arrow. This rig was originally constructed with a 2-door cab, but was rebuilt around 1997 as a four-door. Serial #E 6511-02 is equipped with a 1500-gpm pump and a 500-gallon tank. *Steve Hagy.*

Roll-up doors on apparatus were starting to find their way into American fire stations. Albuquerque, New Mexico operates this rig as Engine 5. It is one of four engines purchased by the A.F.D. during 1991. Equipped with a 1500-gpm pump and a 500-gallon tank, it is serial #E 6587-03. *Eric Hansen.*

Overland Park, Kansas operates this 1991 Arrow. Equipped with a 1500-gpm pump and a 500-gallon tank, it sports a 65-foot Tele-Squrt. Truck 451 has a light bar mounted beneath the windshield for maximum visibility to automobiles. Serial #E 5921. *Eric Hansen.*

Notice the difference in size on the 50-foot Tele-Squrt shown here and the 65-foot job shown on the previous page. This rig for Colonial Heights, Virginia has a 1500-gpm pump and 500-gallon tank and is also a 1991 model. Serial #E 6568. *George Reichhardt.*

Stevens Point, Wisconsin operates several Pierce rigs. Engine 608 is a 1991 Arrow with a 1250-gpm pump and 500-gallon tank. Serial #E 6439. *George Reichhardt.*

Tanker 1105 of the Mitchell Fire Protection District, Illinois has a 1991 Arrow with a 1250-gpm pump and can hold 3,000 gallons of water. This rig is painted white with a lime green stripe. Serial #E 6240. *Dennis Maag.*

A 105-foot aerial is mounted on this 1992 delivery for Barnstable, Massachusetts. Ladder 206 is serial #E 6552. *Neal Van Deusen.*

Brecksville, Ohio has this 1992 Arrow in service as Engine 3. This rig has a 2000-gpm pump and a 750-gallon tank. Notice the exceptionally high-mounted reel for 1 1/2-inch hose. Serial #E 6916. *Dan Martin*.

This 1992 Arrow has a colorful gold stripe to go with the white paint job. A Roto-Ray warning light is mounted on the cab of Engine 8's rig in Clayton County, Georgia. A 1250-gpm pump, 750-gallon water tank, and 40-gallon foam tank are also on this pumper. *Paul Barrett.*

Engine 176 of the Fairview, New York fire department has this lime green Arrow with a white cab roof. Equipped with a 1500-gpm pump and a 500-gallon tank, it is one of a pair purchased in 1992. Serial #E 6771-02. *Neal Van Duesen*.

Park City, Utah has this Pierce Arrow with a 50-foot Tele-Squrt. This rig was delivered in 1992; however, it was rebuilt using the chassis and components from a Mack rig. Engine 1 has a 1500-gpm pump and 500-gallon tank. *Mark Boatwright.*

Pumper-tankers are popular with many departments. Sequim, Washington has this 1992 Arrow carrying 2,500 gallons of water. Serial #E 7172 is also equipped with a 1500-gpm pump. *Bill Hattersley*.

Pierce apparatus helps protect the Kennedy Space Center in Florida. Engine 2 has a 1993 Arrow with a 1250-gpm pump and a 1000-gallon tank. Notice that the booster reel is mounted on the front bumper of this rig. Serial #E 7597. *Jack Connors.*

The Texas Fireman Training School at College Station uses this 1993 Arrow to educate firefighters from the Lone Star state. A 1250-gpm pump, 750-gallon tank, top-mounted pump control panel, and hydraulic ladder rack are among the features of this piece. *Eric Hansen.*

Springfield, Oregon operates a 1993 Arrow as Engine 1. A 50-foot Tele-Squrt, 1500-gpm pump, and a 500-gallon tank are on board serial #E 7377. This department operates with many Pierce rigs that are painted an eye-catching orange tone with a blue reflective stripe. *Bill Hattersley.*

The body of this 1993 rig for Mt. Pleasant, Wisconsin was partially built using diamond plate. This big pumper has a 1500-gpm pump, 750-gallon tank, and a 40-gallon foam tank. Serial #E 7607. *George Reichhardt.*

Columbia, Tennessee has this 1993 delivery in service as Engine 1. Equipped with a 1250-gpm pump and a 750-gallon tank, this lime green rig shares quarters with a Pierce Arrow aerial tower of 1988 vintage. Serial #E 7522. *Steve Hagy.*

East Allen Township, Pennsylvania operates this quint. Delivered in 1993, this rig has a 1750-gpm pump, 500-gallon tank, and 75-foot aerial on board Unit 4621. *Rick Rudisill.*

Grilles were becoming a frequently requested option on Arrows being delivered. This 1993 aerial tower for Little Rock, Arkansas is so equipped. Truck 5 has a 100-foot tower and carries serial #E 7525. *Paul Barrett.*

Snorkels are not sold in the quantities that they were back in the 1960s and 1970s. This 75-foot model is in service as Truck 14 in sunny San Diego, California. Delivered in 1993, it is serial #E 7446. *Chuck Madderom.*

Morton Grove, Illinois operates this heavy rescue constructed on an Arrow chassis, which was acquired in 1993. This rig has a black-over-red paint job that was originated by the Chicago Fire Department and is now in use on apparatus across the United States. Serial #E 7771. *Paul Barrett.*

Many government installations use Pierce apparatus in their firefighting fleets, and the Arrow is very popular among them. The Submarine Base Fire Department of the U.S. Navy in Groton, Connecticut has this 1994 Pierce 105-foot rear-mount aerial in service as Ladder 15. Serial #E 8293. *Mark Redman.*

This Arrow quint can be found way up north in Hibbing, Minnesota. A 1250-gpm pump, 300-gallon tank, and 105-foot aerial are carried on this yellow rig that has been in service since 1994. *Paul Barrett.*

Pike Township at Indianapolis, Indiana also uses yellow as the color for their apparatus. A big 2000-gpm pump is on this 100-foot aerial tower that also carries 150 gallons of water. Serial #E 8427 is a 1994 model. *Steve Hagy.*

Troy, Ohio specified roll-up compartment doors on their Arrow tower. This 1994 delivery is seen in front of the headquarters station there. The rig is equipped with a 1500-gpm pump, 200-gallon tank, and a 100-foot aerial tower. Serial #E 8170 was photographed by Chief John Denney of the Troy F.D.

King County Fire District 2 at Burien, Washington operates this 1994 Arrow as Ladder 244. Serial #E 8158 is painted white with a red stripe and has a 105-foot aerial. A 1500-gpm pump and 200 gallons of water are also on this rig. *Bill Hattersley.*

Engine 3 in Kalamazoo, Michigan has a 1994 Arrow in service. This piece has a 1250-gpm pump, 500-gallon tank, and a 50-foot Tele-Squrt. Roll-up doors are used in combination with standard swing-out doors on the compartments. Serial #E 8114. *Paul Barrett.*

This rig has the same pump, tank, and Tele-Squrt specifications as the Kalamazoo delivery on the previous page, but what a difference in appearance. The U.S. Navy Education & Training Center at Newport, Rhode Island operates serial #E 8717. The lime green paint job, lack of a grille, and a different compartment configuration greatly alter the appearance. This 1994 rig also carries 100 gallons of foam. *Mark Redman.*

The Idaho Falls Fire Department operates this 1995 Arrow as Engine 1. Equipped with a 1250-gpm pump and a 750-gallon tank, this rig also has enclosed booster reels. This is to protect the reels from freezing during those cold, Idaho winters. Serial #E 9329. *Mark Boatwright.*

Fire apparatus delivered today is equipped with a variety of warning devices. Bells, however, are found on only a small percentage of new rigs. Ladder 201 in Carthage, Texas not only has a bell, but is also equipped with a Roto-Ray warning light on the cab. This 1995 acquisition has a 1500-gpm pump, 500-gallon tank, 75-foot aerial, and factory #E 8853. *Eric Hansen.*

The University of Connecticut Health Center at Farmington has this attractive rig on the roster. A 1995 Pierce, it is equipped with a 1500-gpm pump, 750-gallon tank, and a 60-gallon foam tank. Engine 1 is serial #E 9064. *Mark Redman.*

Peru, Illinois is a faithful user of Pierce apparatus. Engine 313 is a 1996 Arrow with a 1250-gpm pump, 1000-gallon tank, and a 30-gallon foam tank. A hydraulic ladder rack is also on this rig. Serial #E 9627. *George Reichhardt.*

Homewood, Alabama uses this 1996 Arrow as Engine 3, which is one of several Pierce rigs on that department's roster. Equipped with a 1250-gpm pump, 300-gallon tank, and 75-foot aerial, this rig is serial #E 9744. *Steve Hagy.*

The U.S. Air Force has purchased a large quantity of these four-wheel drive heavy rescue trucks for its bases in 1996. A 17-foot, non-walk-in style body with roll-up doors was specified. The rig pictured here is Rescue 1 at Mountain Home Air Force Base, Idaho. Serial #E 9596-02. *Mark Boatwright.*

Dennis Maag is a firefighter with the Mehlville, Fire Protection District in suburban St. Louis, Missouri. Engine 1760 of his department is this 1997 Arrow equipped with a 1250-gpm pump and a 500-gallon tank. Dennis' photo of serial #EA 558 shows Mehlville's new black-over-red paint scheme.

The Feasterville Fire Company of Bucks County, Pennsylvania responds with this 1997 Arrow. Ladder 1 has a 105-foot rear-mount aerial. Serial #EA 270. *Rick Rudisill.*

This 1997 Arrow pumper was in service at the Daytona International Speedway in Florida. One of the more unusual features of this rig is that it is equipped with all-around independent suspension. This rig was built with pride by Pierce and has a 1500-gpm pump and a 500-gallon tank. Serial #EA 791 even has checkered flags on the door! *Eric Hansen.*

The U. S. Army at Fort Monmouth, New Jersey has this sharp looking rig in service as Squrt 75-91. A 1997 delivery, a 1250-gpm pump, 500-gallon tank, and 65-foot Tele-Squrt are on board serial #EA 324. This rig also carries Hurst tools, other rescue gear, and is powered by an 8V-92TA Detroit Diesel engine. *Scott Mattson.*

Comstock, Michigan took delivery of this rescue-pumper during 1997. In addition to a 1500-gpm pump and a 500-gallon tank, this rig carries assorted heavy rescue tools. Many pumpers of this type are now being constructed. Serial #EA 843. *Paul Barrett.*

Swimmin' pools, movie stars. Yep, this 100-foot tractor drawn aerial was delivered to the Beverly Hills, California Fire Department. Notice that the aerial is not mounted flat on the trailer, which allows for improved visibility from the tiller compartment. Serial #EB 094 was built in 1998. *Chuck Madderom.*

More Titles from Iconografix:

AMERICAN CULTURE
AMERICAN SERVICE STATIONS 1935-1943 PHOTO ARCHIVE .... ISBN 1-882256-27-1
COCA-COLA: A HISTORY IN PHOTOGRAPHS 1930-1969 .... ISBN 1-882256-46-8
COCA-COLA: ITS VEHICLES IN PHOTOGRAPHS 1930-1969 .... ISBN 1-882256-47-6
PHILLIPS 66 1945-1954 PHOTO ARCHIVE .... ISBN 1-882256-42-5

AUTOMOTIVE
CADILLAC 1948-1964 PHOTO ALBUM .... ISBN 1-882256-83-2
CORVETTE THE EXOTIC EXPERIMENTAL CARS, LUDVIGSEN LIBRARY SERIES .... ISBN 1-58388-017-8
CORVETTE PROTOTYPES & SHOW CARS PHOTO ALBUM .... ISBN 1-882256-77-3
EARLY FORD V-8S 1932-1942 PHOTO ALBUM .... ISBN 1-882256-97-2
IMPERIAL 1955-1963 PHOTO ARCHIVE .... ISBN 1-882256-22-0
IMPERIAL 1964-1968 PHOTO ARCHIVE .... ISBN 1-882256-23-9
LINCOLN MOTOR CARS 1920-1942 PHOTO ARCHIVE .... ISBN 1-882256-57-3
LINCOLN MOTOR CARS 1946-1960 PHOTO ARCHIVE .... ISBN 1-882256-58-1
PACKARD MOTOR CARS 1935-1942 PHOTO ARCHIVE .... ISBN 1-882256-44-1
PACKARD MOTOR CARS 1946-1958 PHOTO ARCHIVE .... ISBN 1-882256-45-X
PONTIAC DREAM CARS, SHOW CARS & PROTOTYPES 1928-1998 PHOTO ALBUM .... ISBN 1-882256-93-X
PONTIAC FIREBIRD TRANS-AM 1969-1999 PHOTO ALBUM .... ISBN 1-882256-95-6
PORSCHE 356 1948-1965 PHOTO ALBUM .... ISBN 1-882256-85-9
STUDEBAKER 1933-1942 PHOTO ARCHIVE .... ISBN 1-882256-24-7
STUDEBAKER 1946-1958 PHOTO ARCHIVE .... ISBN 1-882256-25-5

EMERGENCY VEHICLES
AMERICAN LAFRANCE 700 SERIES 1945-1952 PHOTO ARCHIVE .... ISBN 1-882256-90-5
AMERICAN LAFRANCE 700 & 800 SERIES 1953-1958 PHOTO ARCHIVE .... ISBN 1-882256-91-3
AMERICAN LAFRANCE 900 SERIES 1958-1964 PHOTO ARCHIVE .... ISBN 1-58388-002-X
CLASSIC AMERICAN AMBULANCES 1900-1979 PHOTO ARCHIVE .... ISBN 1-882256-94-8
CLASSIC AMERICAN FUNERAL VEHICLES 1900-1980 PHOTO ARCHIVE .... ISBN 1-58388-016-X
FIRE CHIEF CARS 1900-1997 PHOTO ALBUM .... ISBN 1-882256-87-5
LOS ANGELES CITY FIRE APPARATUS 1953 - 1999 PHOTO ARCHIVE .... ISBN 1-58388-012-7
MACK® MODEL B FIRE TRUCKS 1954-1966 PHOTO ARCHIVE* .... ISBN 1-882256-62-X
MACK MODEL C FIRE TRUCKS 1957-1967 PHOTO ARCHIVE* .... ISBN 1-58388-014-3
MACK MODEL CF FIRE TRUCKS 1967-1981 PHOTO ARCHIVE* .... ISBN 1-882256-63-8
MACK MODEL L FIRE TRUCKS 1940-1954 PHOTO ARCHIVE* .... ISBN 1-882256-86-7
PIERCE ARROW FIRE APPARATUS 1979-1998 PHOTO ARCHIVE .... ISBN 1-58388-023-2
SEAGRAVE 70TH ANNIVERSARY SERIES PHOTO ARCHIVE .... ISBN 1-58388-001-1
VOLUNTEER & RURAL FIRE APPARATUS PHOTO GALLERY .... ISBN 1-58388-005-4

RACING
GT40 PHOTO ARCHIVE .... ISBN 1-882256-64-6
INDY CARS OF THE 1950s, LUDVIGSEN LIBRARY SERIES .... ISBN 1-58388-018-6
JUAN MANUEL FANGIO WORLD CHAMPION DRIVER SERIES PHOTO ALBUM ...... ISBN 1-58388-008-9
LE MANS 1950: THE BRIGGS CUNNINGHAM CAMPAIGN PHOTO ARCHIVE .... ISBN 1-882256-21-2
LOTUS RACE CARS 1961-1994 PHOTO ALBUM .... ISBN 1-882256-84-0
MARIO ANDRETTI WORLD CHAMPION DRIVER SERIES PHOTO ALBUM .... ISBN 1-58388-009-7
SEBRING 12-HOUR RACE 1970 PHOTO ARCHIVE .... ISBN 1-882256-20-4
VANDERBILT CUP RACE 1936 & 1937 PHOTO ARCHIVE .... ISBN 1-882256-66-2
WILLIAMS 1969-1998 30 YEARS OF GRAND PRIX RACING PHOTO ALBUM .... ISBN 1-58388-000-3

RAILWAYS
CHICAGO, ST. PAUL, MINNEAPOLIS & OMAHA RAILWAY 1880-1940 PHOTO ARCHIVE ...... ISBN 1-882256-67-0
CHICAGO & NORTH WESTERN RAILWAY 1975-1995 PHOTO ARCHIVE .... ISBN 1-882256-76-X
GREAT NORTHERN RAILWAY 1945-1970 PHOTO ARCHIVE .... ISBN 1-882256-56-5
GREAT NORTHERN RAILWAY 1945-1970 VOL 2 PHOTO ARCHIVE .... ISBN 1-882256-79-4
MILWAUKEE ROAD 1850-1960 PHOTO ARCHIVE .... ISBN 1-882256-61-1
SOO LINE 1975-1992 PHOTO ARCHIVE .... ISBN 1-882256-68-9
TRAINS OF THE TWIN PORTS, DULUTH-SUPERIOR IN THE 1950s PHOTO ARCHIVE ...... ISBN 1-58388-003-8
TRAINS OF THE CIRCUS 1872-1956 PHOTO ARCHIVE .... ISBN 1-58388-024-0
WISCONSIN CENTRAL LIMITED 1987-1996 PHOTO ARCHIVE .... ISBN 1-882256-75-1
WISCONSIN CENTRAL RAILWAY 1871-1909 PHOTO ARCHIVE .... ISBN 1-882256-78-6

*This product is sold under license from Mack Trucks, Inc. Mack is a registered Trademark of Mack Trucks, Inc. All rights reserved.

TRUCKS & BUSES
BEVERAGE TRUCKS 1910-1975 PHOTO ARCHIVE .... ISBN 1-882256-60-3
BROCKWAY TRUCKS 1948-1961 PHOTO ARCHIVE* .... ISBN 1-882256-55-7
DODGE PICKUPS 1939-1978 PHOTO ALBUM .... ISBN 1-882256-82-4
DODGE POWER WAGONS 1940-1980 PHOTO ARCHIVE .... ISBN 1-882256-89-1
DODGE POWER WAGON PHOTO HISTORY .... ISBN 1-58388-019-4
DODGE TRUCKS 1929-1947 PHOTO ARCHIVE .... ISBN 1-882256-36-0
DODGE TRUCKS 1948-1960 PHOTO ARCHIVE .... ISBN 1-882256-37-9
THE GENERAL MOTORS NEW LOOK BUS PHOTO ARCHIVE .... ISBN 1-58388-007-0
JEEP 1941-2000 PHOTO ARCHIVE .... ISBN 1-58388-021-6
LOGGING TRUCKS 1915-1970 PHOTO ARCHIVE .... ISBN 1-882256-59-X
MACK MODEL AB PHOTO ARCHIVE* .... ISBN 1-882256-18-2
MACK AP SUPER-DUTY TRUCKS 1926-1938 PHOTO ARCHIVE* .... ISBN 1-882256-54-9
MACK BUSES 1900-1960 PHOTO ARCHIVE* .... ISBN 1-58388-020-8
MACK MODEL B 1953-1966 VOL 1 PHOTO ARCHIVE* .... ISBN 1-882256-19-0
MACK MODEL B 1953-1966 VOL 2 PHOTO ARCHIVE* .... ISBN 1-882256-34-4
MACK EB-EC-ED-EE-EF-EG-DE 1936-1951 PHOTO ARCHIVE* .... ISBN 1-882256-29-8
MACK EH-EJ-EM-EQ-ER-ES 1936-1950 PHOTO ARCHIVE* .... ISBN 1-882256-39-5
MACK FC-FCSW-NW 1936-1947 PHOTO ARCHIVE* .... ISBN 1-882256-28-X
MACK FG-FH-FJ-FK-FN-FP-FT-FW 1937-1950 PHOTO ARCHIVE* .... ISBN 1-882256-35-2
MACK LF-LH-LJ-LM-LT 1940-1956 PHOTO ARCHIVE* .... ISBN 1-882256-38-7
MACK TRUCKS PHOTO GALLERY* .... ISBN 1-882256-88-3
NEW CAR CARRIERS 1910-1998 PHOTO ALBUM .... ISBN 1-882256-98-0
PLYMOUTH COMMERCIAL VEHICLES PHOTO ARCHIVE .... ISBN 1-58388-004-6
STUDEBAKER TRUCKS 1927-1940 PHOTO ARCHIVE .... ISBN 1-882256-40-9
STUDEBAKER TRUCKS 1941-1964 PHOTO ARCHIVE .... ISBN 1-882256-41-7
WHITE TRUCKS 1900-1937 PHOTO ARCHIVE .... ISBN 1-882256-80-8

TRACTORS & CONSTRUCTION EQUIPMENT
CASE TRACTORS 1912-1959 PHOTO ARCHIVE .... ISBN 1-882256-32-8
CATERPILLAR PHOTO GALLERY .... ISBN 1-882256-70-0
CATERPILLAR POCKET GUIDE THE TRACK-TYPE TRACTORS 1925-1957 ...... ISBN 1-58388-022-4
CATERPILLAR D-2 & R-2 PHOTO ARCHIVE .... ISBN 1-882256-99-9
CATERPILLAR D 8 1933-1974 INCLUDING DIESEL 75 & RD-8 PHOTO ARCHIVE ..... ISBN 1-882256-96-4
CATERPILLAR MILITARY TRACTORS VOLUME 1 PHOTO ARCHIVE .... ISBN 1-882256-16-6
CATERPILLAR MILITARY TRACTORS VOLUME 2 PHOTO ARCHIVE .... ISBN 1-882256-17-4
CATERPILLAR SIXTY PHOTO ARCHIVE .... ISBN 1-882256-05-0
CATERPILLAR TEN INCLUDING 7C FIFTEEN & HIGH FIFTEEN PHOTO ARCHIVE ..... ISBN 1-58388-011-9
CATERPILLAR THIRTY 2ND ED. INC. BEST THIRTY, 6G THIRTY & R-4 PHOTO ARCHIVE ...... ISBN 1-58388-006-2
CLETRAC AND OLIVER CRAWLERS PHOTO ARCHIVE .... ISBN 1-882256-43-3
ERIE SHOVEL PHOTO ARCHIVE .... ISBN 1-882256-69-7
FARMALL CUB PHOTO ARCHIVE .... ISBN 1-882256-71-9
FARMALL F- SERIES PHOTO ARCHIVE .... ISBN 1-882256-02-6
FARMALL MODEL H PHOTO ARCHIVE .... ISBN 1-882256-03-4
FARMALL MODEL M PHOTO ARCHIVE .... ISBN 1-882256-15-8
FARMALL REGULAR PHOTO ARCHIVE .... ISBN 1-882256-14-X
FARMALL SUPER SERIES PHOTO ARCHIVE .... ISBN 1-882256-49-2
FORDSON 1917-1928 PHOTO ARCHIVE .... ISBN 1-882256-33-6
HART-PARR PHOTO ARCHIVE .... ISBN 1-882256-08-5
HOLT TRACTORS PHOTO ARCHIVE .... ISBN 1-882256-10-7
INTERNATIONAL TRACTRACTOR PHOTO ARCHIVE .... ISBN 1-882256-48-4
INTERNATIONAL TD CRAWLERS 1933-1962 PHOTO ARCHIVE .... ISBN 1-882256-72-7
JOHN DEERE MODEL A PHOTO ARCHIVE .... ISBN 1-882256-12-3
JOHN DEERE MODEL B PHOTO ARCHIVE .... ISBN 1-882256-01-8
JOHN DEERE MODEL D PHOTO ARCHIVE .... ISBN 1-882256-00-X
JOHN DEERE 30 SERIES PHOTO ARCHIVE .... ISBN 1-882256-13-1
MINNEAPOLIS-MOLINE U-SERIES PHOTO ARCHIVE .... ISBN 1-882256-07-7
OLIVER TRACTORS PHOTO ARCHIVE .... ISBN 1-882256-09-3
RUSSELL GRADERS PHOTO ARCHIVE .... ISBN 1-882256-11-5
TWIN CITY TRACTOR PHOTO ARCHIVE .... ISBN 1-882256-06-9

All Iconografix books are available from direct mail specialty book dealers and bookstores worldwide, or can be ordered from the publisher. For book trade and distribution information or to add your name to our mailing list contact:

Iconografix, PO Box 446, Hudson, Wisconsin, 54016   Telephone: (715) 381-9755, (800) 289-3504 (USA), Fax: (715) 381-9756

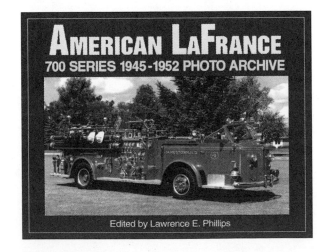
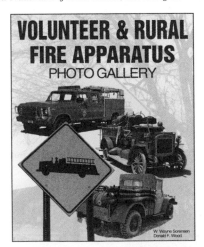
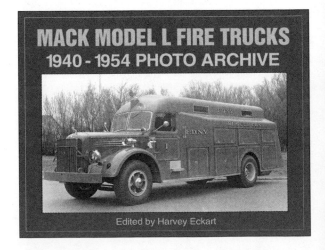